Mercy
in the
Fathers
of the
Church

Mercy
in the
Fathers
of the
Church

PONTIFICAL COUNCIL FOR THE PROMOTION
OF THE NEW EVANGELIZATION

Jubilee of Mercy
2015-2016

Our Sunday Visitor Publishing Division
Our Sunday Visitor, Inc.
Huntington, Indiana 46750

Copyright © 2015 Pontifical Council for the Promotion of the New Evangelization Vatican City

Published 2015 by Our Sunday Visitor Publishing Division

20 19 18 17 16 15   1 2 3 4 5 6 7 8 9

Our Sunday Visitor Publishing Division, Our Sunday Visitor, Inc., 200 Noll Plaza, Huntington, IN 46750; 1-800-348-2440

ISBN: 978-1-61278-978-1 (Inventory No. T1738)
eISBN: 978-1-61278-986-6
LCCN: 2015948392

Translation: Andrew Spannaus
Cover design: Lindsey Riesen
Cover art: Shutterstock; Pontifical Council for Promotion of the New Evangelization
Interior design: Sherri Hoffman

PRINTED IN THE UNITED STATES OF AMERICA

TABLE OF CONTENTS

INTRODUCTION

The reference to mercy is the true common thread in Christian history. There have indeed been moments in which certain historical events have clouded the visibility of mercy, to the point of overshadowing it; various wars and conquests of territory, scandals, and episodes of violence have pushed God's tenderness off into a corner. Yet that has never succeeded in eliminating mercy from the life of the Church. It would be easy to show that it was precisely in these dark periods of our history that incredibly saintly figures emerged that demonstrated God's goodness in the testimony of their lives.

We preserve the memory of saints who became famous because the institutions they founded remain as a concrete sign of their charity. We cannot, however, forget the hundreds of thousands of simple men and women, whose "names are written in heaven" (Lk 10:20), who with their daily loyalty to the Gospel brought Christ's teachings to life, giving voice to the many works of mercy.

The Fathers of the Church represent an important chapter of this history. Therefore, we have created a short anthology of passages on mercy to show how the theme of mercy marked their lives and teachings. From this perspective the reference to the parable of the good Samaritan remains a constant point of reference for many of the Fathers. An important reference in the West is offered by St. Augustine, the true poet of mercy. Observing the scene of Jesus on the cross, in the presence of the thief to whom he promised: "Today you will be with me in paradise," St. Augustine commented: "The Lord, when he said to him: 'Remember me;' but when? 'When you arrive in your kingdom,' immediately responded: 'I say to you that today you will be with me in paradise.' Mercy granted that which misery had delayed" (*Sermon* 67, 4.7).

This pastoral instrument is divided into three parts: the first part offers a general introduction to the theme, showing how mercy cuts across the teachings of these great masters of the early centuries of our history. In the second part, due to the importance of the theme, there is a brief introduction to St. Augustine with some of the most significant passages of his works. Last, in the third part, there is a collection of certain passages from the Fathers of the Eastern and Western Churches to assist in reflection and prayer in this Jubilee Year. They can easily be used in catechesis, lessons, and prayer. A vision emerges that touches every aspect of Christian life and allows for recovering what is truly a hidden treasure. The Pontifical Council for the Promotion of the New Evangelization is grateful to H.E. Monsignor Enrico dal Covolo and to Father Vittorino Grossi for having contributed to the composition of this text. We hope that their abilities and labors will be rewarded with the knowledge that a great number of Christians will have access to texts that are often unknown, to sustain and solidify their faith.

✠ Rino Fisichella
President, Pontifical Council for the
Promotion of the New Evangelization

CHAPTER I

Mercy: The Christian Lifestyle

The extraordinary jubilee that will begin on December 8, 2015, on the fiftieth anniversary of the Second Vatican Council (1962-1965), is a strong invitation to celebrate, live, and praise the mercy of the Father revealed by the Lord Jesus and spread in our hearts by the Holy Spirit (see Rom 5:5). In fact, the motto of the Jubilee Year, as indicated by Pope Francis in the papal bull *Misericordiae Vultus*, is "Merciful like the Father," referencing *poets of divine mercy* with desire, works, thoughts, and all of our lives — that is, the prophets and the saints, and all of the Christian generations since the origins of the Church. The Fathers of the Church occupy a special place in the ranks of those poets of mercy.

The invitation to be merciful "even as your Father is merciful" (Lk 6:36) was often translated by the Fathers of the Church as an invitation to true perfection, evangelical perfection — that is, the common calling of all Christians to sainthood (see *Lumen Gentium,* 40). For the Fathers, in their experience and their thinking, the invitation to mercy and to perfection are strictly linked, because the pastors and doctors in the early centuries of

Christianity always recognized themselves and the entire pilgrim Church as needing the merciful goodness of a forgiving God. Therefore, to be Christian, and thus similar to Christ, the Perfect One, is possible; and it is possible to the greatest extent, if one accepts divine mercy and becomes a merciful person.

Today, the Church feels the need to transmit the Gospel of mercy, and to that end the lesson of the Fathers and of the always-living tradition of the Church is an essential element to approach, contemplate, and transmit the mystery of mercy in all of its wealth, the source of true joy.

The Fathers and the non-Christian Ancient World

It is well-known that from the beginning the ancient Christian world measured itself not only with biblical culture, but also with the culture of the pagan world. Ancient philosophy had dealt broadly with the question of mercy, but the judgment on the issue was always very controversial.

In the most ancient Greek thinking, which is broadly reflected in the Homeric poems, mercy is considered one of the noblest virtues. As Giacomo Leopardi (1798-1837) observed in his book *Zibaldone*, the *Iliad*, compared to the later epic poems, continues to interest us after "as much as twenty-seven centuries," due to the "strange and almost absurd fact that during ferocious times Homer had compassion play such a role in his poem," and that this falls "almost solely on the enemies of his Greek countrymen to whom he wrote, who did not particularly value generosity toward the enemy, but rather appreciated the opposite quality." In the *Iliad*, the poet teaches the new feeling of compassion while he sketches heroes who know it not, and therefore he composes not only "the most sentimental, actually the only sentimental poem" among all of the epic poems, but "also the most Christian poem, " according to Leopardi.

With Plato (428-348 B.C.), but above all with Stoicism,

which considered mercy as a disease of the soul — *aegritudo animi* — philosophy had considered compassion and mercy equivalent to a human weakness (see *Apology*, 34c). For the philosopher, compassion and mercy are opposed to conduct guided by reason and the search for justice, which for the ancients was essentially retributive justice: "To each what he deserves" (*suum cuique*).

The question of the relationship between justice and mercy runs through all subsequent thought, including Christian thought, with different outcomes that over time have led to losing the authentic sense of mercy, especially in theological thinking, as many have noted, even in recent times. The issue of the relationship between justice and mercy was strongly recalled by Pope Francis in *Misericordiae Vultus* (20), and definitely deserves to be examined further during the Jubilee Year, including in light of the lessons of the Fathers. Isaac of Nineveh (sixth century), at the end of the patristic age in a strict sense, wrote as if a summary: "If the merciful be not even above justice, he is not merciful" (*Mystic Treatise*, 4).

Returning to the classical tradition, for Aristotle (384-322 B.C.) compassion was not considered a virtue, but nevertheless he had a positive conception of it: in his view the experience of undeserved suffering moves the soul of one who views it, because such an evil could affect him as well. This leads the viewer to act, expressing solidarity with a person who suffers unjustly (see *Rhetoric*, 1385b). For the Stoics, the feeling produced in the human soul by compassion is absolutely irreconcilable with the principles of the rational domain of sentiment, with the self-sufficiency, indifference, and imperturbability to which the followers of the *Stoa* were called. This does not diminish the fact that Stoic philosophy broadly appreciated the exercise of clemency (*clementia*), philanthropy (*humanitas*), and the benevolent willingness to help other human beings (*benignitas*) (see Seneca, *On Clemency*, 2.6).

Cicero (106-43 B.C.), who would later often be cited by St. Augustine and by many other Fathers of the Latin West, despite using the Stoic definition of mercy/compassion as a disease of the soul, also expressed high consideration for merciful men in his writings. In the oration *Pro Murena*, distancing himself from the excesses of Stoicism in his adversary Cato and appealing to the traditional Roman distrust of Greek thought, he criticizes Zeno of Citium (c. 335-c. 263 B.C.) and the Orthodox Stoics, who argued that "the wise man is never moved by compassion, he never forgives anyone for a sin, no one is compassionate except for the fool and the superficial man."

In any event, we are generally far from the shocking evangelical message of God who becomes man for mercy, as noted vividly by Origen (d. A.D. 254): "Man, therefore, is made according to the likeness of his image, and for this reason our Savior, who is the image of God, moved with compassion for man who had been made according to his likeness, seeing him, his own image having been laid aside, to have put on the image of the evil one ... assumed the image of man and came to him" (*Homily on Genesis*, 1.13.54s).

In an even more shocking manner, the Doctor from Alexandria writes: "The Father himself is not without suffering. When he is prayed to, he has pity and mercy, he suffers from love and empathizes with the sentiments he could not have, given the greatness of his nature, and on account of us he endures human sufferings" (*Homily on Ezekiel*, 6.6.119). Origen also established the dogma of divine impassivity, but the case of mercy seems radically different to him.

Mercy between Holy Scripture and the Fathers
In the comprehension of the great mystery of God's boundless

love for man, the Fathers of the Church began with the reading of holy Scripture, the rules of Christian life, meditated, proclaimed, celebrated, and lived in the Church. Scripture occupied and continues to occupy an absolutely fundamental place in the life of the community, and must inform every action of life, from liturgy to doctrine to discipline, both collectively and individually. We can certainly state that the entire life of the Christian community is guided by the interpretation of holy Scripture: its study represented the authentic foundation for Christian culture in the early centuries of the Church.

At the heart of the message transmitted by Scripture, the biblical God is often defined with the combination of being patient and merciful (see Ps 145), and in the history of salvation his goodness often prevails over the destruction and punishment announced due to the faithlessness of human beings. Because of those threats, contained in the pages of the Old Testament, certain heresies arose in ethno-Christian environments and radical anti-Jewish Paulinism that set the God of the Old Testament sharply in contrast with the good Father revealed by Jesus.

In particular, we recall the heresy of Marcion of Sinope (second century), who, thanks to considerable resources and rich donations, sought to seize the attention of the Roman Church, of which he wanted to climb the rungs of leadership. When his plans were revealed, Marcion was quickly convicted, and in 144 he was expelled by the community of Rome, which returned a donation it had received from him amounting to 200,000 *sesterces* (an ancient Roman coin). This large sum would have been useful for the Roman church, which had immediately distinguished itself for its active charity in favor of the poor (*egeni*), as attested to by Justin Martyr, who speaks of Sunday collections to help the poor. The return of the 200,000 sesterces must have been particularly difficult, but it reminds us that *charity* and *truth* are inseparable for the Christian community, and *together* they are the manifestation of divine mercy.

In the tradition of the Catholic Doctors, such as the great African master Tertullian (c. 155-c. 230) and St. Irenaeus (c. 135-c. 202) — one of the greatest early Christian authors, educated in Asia Minor before becoming the Bishop of Lyon in Gaul — the unity of the two Testaments and the sole revelation of divine mercy for humanity are identified decisively through sophisticated tools for interpreting Scripture. Tertullian states that the God revealed to Moses, the "merciful and charitable God, slow to anger and rich in love and loyalty," is the same "Father of mercies and God of all comfort" (2 Cor 1:3) of the New Testament (see *Against Marcion*, 5.11).

The Fathers of the Church, even in the most difficult and harshest pages of the Judaic Scripture, were always able to grasp, with the insight and spiritual intelligence that set them apart, the revelation of Christ that is hidden in the Old Testament like the treasure in a field of the Gospel of Matthew (see 13:44).

Mercy as "Misery" and "Heart"

Mercy is a very ancient Latin word and, during its long history in those who have experienced it, has acquired delicate meanings from the many nuances of language of the two terms which make it up: "misery" and "heart." In *Confessions*, St. Augustine specifies: usually, misery is defined as one's own suffering, while suffering for others is defined as mercy (see 3, 2.2).

In Greek, the language of the New Testament, the word for mercy is *eleos* — a word that is familiar to us thanks to the prayer *Kyrie eleison*, the invocation of the Lord's mercy. This in turn is a translation of the Hebrew word *hésèd*, one of the most beautiful biblical words, that stresses the faithfulness of God's mercy for each man. That is why it is often translated very simply as "love," or "the faithfulness of God's love," for humanity.

The Greek *eleos* also translates another Hebrew term, *rahamîm*, which indicates a *hésèd* (faith in love) full of emotions, signifying the maternal bosom. God's faithfulness in his mercy was expressly celebrated in the Israelites' prayer assemblies using Psalms 117 and 135.

The emotion of mercy is recorded by the Gospels with reference to Jesus such as at the Last Supper where it is noted that the beloved disciple rested his head close to Jesus' breast (see Jn 13:23); actually, the text says that he rested his head on the Lord's maternal womb, the place where we are continually generated, expressed by the affection of the mother for her child (see Is 49:15). In the parable of the forgiving father, again we note that when the father saw his son returning to him, his felt compassion in his maternal/paternal womb (see Lk 15:20).

In Latin, the word "mercy" consists of the two terms *misery* and *heart*. "Misery" expresses that extreme smallness that asks for pity, compassion, and commiseration implored by one who is greatly anguished. Therefore, "misery" speaks of an indigence that threatens the very existence of the person in that state, because he is forced to live at the margins of human life and is barely able to breathe life. The other term, combined with that of misery, is the heart. Misery, approached by the heart, from the Latin root *urere* (which means to burn), is destroyed as if overcome by a fire. So when the heart detects misery present in a person, it does not judge it, it burns it, it destroys it. And this is mercy. When a heart approaches you, you feel the heat; it burns your misery, meaning that negativity which has enveloped you, and you feel the heat of the person who embraces you, who loves you because he does not give importance to your misery. The misery is no more; it has been burned. It is the miracle produced by the merciful heart. The "heart" is the center of the most intimate and true area of every human being. For that reason the "heart" is considered the center of feelings, the sentiments of joy, pain, love, serenity, or anxiety, that impenetrable place of evaluation of each of our consciences.

The union of the two terms thus becomes "mercy"; the loving look full of compassion, of God and of the creature, that freely comes down on misery, comes to rescue, and cancels it with its heart. For this reason mercy is born, lives, takes nourishment, and manifests itself between forgiveness and the affection that embraces you. Living one's days with truth is simply a pilgrimage in search of the place of the heart, that furnace able to burn any misery and produce mercy. The word "mercy" thus indicates a human heart ready to intervene when it recognizes a poverty that is provoking the death of a life; and it also indicates that a misery, that had taken possession of someone, is about to end, because it will be burned by a heart that has recognized it. Of course, man's mercy is limited, as is his heart, but God's mercy is as immense as his existence. Christian mercy can be encountered because it has a face and a name — it is called "Jesus Christ." In him mercy is the face of the Father's love for each human creature.

The Education of Christians to Mercy

From the time of their birth, Christians are continuously urged by their pastors to be merciful, producing works of mercy in their daily experiences. At the time of the Fathers of the Church, during the period of the catechumenate, Christians were educated with the Our Father prayer to be capable of mercy. That education was based on the conscience of human beings who are born and live their existence surrounded by areas of darkness. Those areas pervade human nature in a situation where the good is difficult, where sin normally expresses itself. Those dark areas, in which human beings are born, become manifest and aggressive with growth: they feel your heart seduced, they feel that your best aspirations are at times corrupted. Indeed, conscience is unable to conceal its torment from the human creature, shaken as it is by that continuous and simultaneous reverberation of values and disvalues inside, of the sense of good and evil. An uneasiness that, in other words, belongs to life: to the life of the individual as to social life and the very life of the Church. The latter gathers people of any language and extraction called by the hope given to them by the revelation of God's mercy. Thanks to that mercy, they can face the difficulties that undermine a loving life together with one's fellow people, and also live the hope of one day being freed from the spiral of temptation by evil in its thousand shades: from discouragement in the meaning of one's existence and in faith in others, to the point of not bearing living in its presence.

Christian education of mercy, in terms of communal life, translates into relationships of mutual help in freeing one another from the evil encountered daily, in not lingering more than necessary in mutually judging one another negatively, in relating to one's fellow humans living with mercy. If our neighbor sins in our regard and we respond at the same level, we forget the gift of mercy, and, as if we had returned to being pagan, we sin as well. Only mutual mercy saves us.

At the time of the Fathers of the Church, those who asked to become Christians were educated to gain consciousness of a common reality of the difficulty we encounter in the world. In this manner the individuals were helped to realize that they were all poor, because they were all torn by the same injury, and as a result they all needed the same mercy. When evil is not thrown on a person, it does not add up, it does not multiply, it loses its destructive force, it becomes a limit as in its negative reality: the absence of good only momentarily, but ready to return to its place. So people no longer act under the forces of evil judging one another, hating one another, killing one another; rather they look at one another and discover that they are all sinners, and they pray together: "Forgive us our debts."

In the patristic era, the tradition of the Church of Rome was not to limit its charitable actions to only its territory and to assisting Roman Christians with difficulties away from their community. Rome realized what St. Ignatius of Antioch (d.c. 107) said of it, that it "presided in charity." St. Dionysius of Corinth (d.c. 175), in writing to Pope Soter (r. 166-175) on traditional Roman solidarity, states: "From the beginning it has been your practice to do good to all the brethren in various ways, and to send contributions to many churches in every city. Thus relieving the want of the needy, and making provision for the brethren in the mines by the gifts which you have sent from the beginning, you Romans keep up the hereditary customs of the Romans, which your blessed bishop Soter has not only maintained, but also added to, furnishing an abundance of supplies to the saints" (see Eusebius, *Church History*, 4.23).

These statements on the charity of the Roman Church are confirmed by ample testimony from other provinces of the Roman Empire: for example, Bishop Dionysius of Alexandria (c. 190-c. 265) left us praise of Pope Stephen (r. 254-257), because in the name of the Church of Rome he regularly sent abundant resources and assistance to the Churches of Syria and Arabia (see Eusebius, *Church History*, 7, 5.2). There were truly many forms of Christian solidarity, of the communities of Rome and of other cities in the empire, often praised even by pagan authors, such as Lucian of Samosata (d. 180), the Emperor Julian (d. 363), and others.

Julian, called the Apostate, who was very familiar with the many forms of the Church's charitable activities, wanted to establish them in the pagan community as well, alongside a modification of traditional religion based on the Christian experience. Tertullian and other ancient authors state that alms, the attention to the needy and the poor, and all works of spiritual and bodily mercy that show a merciful heart, make Christian men and women superior to pagans (see *Apologeticum*, 42.8).

Merely to give an idea of the active charity at the time of the Fathers, we list some of the works that were close to the hearts of the bishops and the Christian communities: help for Christians who were incarcerated or sentenced to various types of forced labor in the early centuries, and then to prisoners in general; the redemption of prostitutes; the redemption of prisoners; aid to the victims of usury; burial for everyone; care for widows and orphans; care for the sick; hospitality for strangers (works of mercy that in the *Shepard of Hermas* are considered the characteristics that make bishops saintly and just men).

In *Against Marcion*, when Tertullian comments on the passage from the prophet Hosea, "I desire mercy and not sacrifice" (Hos 6:6), these two senses of mercy are constantly present: that received from God and that practiced by Christians (see *Against Marcion*, 2, 11.2; 13.5; 17.2; 4, 17.8; 18.9; 20.4). In many Christian authors, synonyms are used for mercy such as *pietas*, *humanitas*, and other terms that have a very ancient and rich classical tradition — as we saw in the case of Seneca — and that Christianity restored and amplified. According to Lactantius (c. 240-c. 320), a learned orator who was converted and then became the tutor of the imperial children of Constantine, mercy is the companion of justice, one addressed in particular to human beings, and the other to God (see *The Divine Institutes*, 6.10). But it would be impossible to return anything to God, if he had first not given everything freely to man, if he had not loved man first, despite man's unworthiness and his inability to turn to the fatherly goodness of God. Another anonymous author from the fourth century, known as Ambrosiaster, writes, "This is the true wealth of God's mercy, that even when we did not seek it, mercy was revealed through his will" (*Comm. Eph*, 2.4).

In the merciful visage of Christ, according to the doctors of the original Church, we can see that divine mercy for man the sinner. Indeed, in charity, mercy, and forgiveness practiced toward one's neighbor, Origen invited his readers to discern the image of God (see *On First Principles*, 4.10). St. Augustine often says that the Christian can contemplate God himself, can see the vision of the Trinity, the immense mystery that one day he will be called on to see and contemplate "face to face" (1 Cor 13:12), only in active charity toward one's neighbor. Augustine says: "You see the Trinity, if you see love" (*On the Trinity*, 8, 8.12).

Jesus' mission is to reveal and communicate to human beings the completeness of the love that is God's life, God himself that is *Love*, as John teaches us (see 1 Jn 4:8-16). Jesus' entire life is an expression of this Love that is given freely, until the ultimate sacrifice on the cross. St. Cyril, Bishop of Alexandria, recalls that mercy is an attribute of divine nature itself, and invites his readers to impress it well in their minds (see *Commentary on Luke, Homily* 29).

The signs that Jesus the Lord performs toward a tired and exhausted humanity, of sinners, poor, outcasts, the sick and suffering, tell us of God's mercy. All of these signs, carried out in many episodes of the Gospel, show how Jesus felt compassion for the lost crowds that followed him and that he worried about them, and with only a few loaves of bread and fish he fed them (see Mt 14:13-21).

The Fathers were always certain to distinguish very carefully between the divine and the human attributes of the Son of God. In the numerous passages in which Jesus is moved by situations of difficultly and suffering in those he meets, his true humanity stands out, and to defend the divinity of the Son of God they use what is shown in the miracles. In short, the divinity that we cannot see is shown through the concrete signs that are before everyone's eyes, as in the case of the multiplication of the bread. However, they also stress Jesus' compassion for the crowd that follows him, his amenability, and the donation that the Lord makes of himself in the economy of salvation. An Eastern author from the fourth century writes, "He was never idle and inactive in the world, but always working to feed everyone without taking anything for himself" (Eusebius of Emesa, *Homily* 8.12).

The Fathers interpret the multiplication of the bread as a sign of the arrival of the Messiah who nourishes his people. Allegorically, the five loaves of bread are often interpreted as the food of the Old Testament, in particular the five books of the Law (the Pentateuch), while the two fish represent the Prophets and John: this is what we read, for example, in Hilary of Poitiers (315-367) (see his *Commentary on Matthew* 14.19). St. Ambrose (c. 340-397) ventures into rather audacious allegories (see *Exposition on the Gospel of Luke* 6.79-80). There are also interpretations that obviously refer to the Eucharistic food.

The miracle of the mercy of Christ, moved by the hungry crowd, does not end with the multiplication: the mercy received spreads and accrues to the benefit of those who give without reservations, as Christ did. There were in fact twelve baskets left over. Thus St. Cyril of Alexandria (370-444) asks: "And what do we infer from this? A plain assurance that hospitality receives a rich recompense from God. The disciples offered five loaves: but after a multitude thus large had been satisfied, there was gathered for each one of them a basketful of fragments. Let nothing therefore prevent those who are willing from receiving strangers.... Let no one say, 'I do not possess suitable means; what I can do is altogether trifling and insufficient for many.' Receive strangers, my beloved; overcome that unreadiness which wins no reward: for the Savior will multiply your little many times beyond expectation" (*Commentary on Luke, Homily* 48).

This interpretation is particularly and dramatically relevant today considering the starving crowds of migrants who, before our eyes, attempt to flee from conflicts and misery, for which only justice joined with mercy can lead to a lasting positive outcome.

Due to his compassionate and merciful love, Jesus heals the poor and feels compassion for the widow in Nain, reviving her son (see Lk 7:11-17). Commenting on these miracles, the Fathers cannot merely discuss Jesus' mercy that forgives, heals, and restores life. Their view is profoundly ecclesiastical, and sees in the woman the image of the community of believers that lives in and spreads the love of Christ, the Bride of Christ, that is moved by the plights of men and women and devotes itself to aiding people with the grace of the sacraments, with forgiveness and also with works of spiritual and bodily mercy. The mother grieving for the loss of her child is the Church that weeps for the sins of the children that it generated in the womb of the baptismal pool. It intervenes for each of us, as if we were its only children, and it weeps, writes St. Ambrose, until each of its children rise during the funeral procession and meet the tomb and eternal death (see *Exposition on the Gospel of Luke* 5.92).

After having freed the man in Gerasenes from the demon, Jesus gave him this mission: "Go home to your friends, and tell them how much the Lord has done for you, and how he has had mercy on you" (Mk 5:19). In this case as well the unanimous comment of the early teachers of Christianity shows that, once the remission of sins is obtained, all the faithful have the duty to allow others to participate in the gifts received and thus to place themselves at the service of the Gospel and the spread of the kingdom of God (see Bede the Venerable, *Commentary on Mark* 2).

Matthew's calling is also included in the realm of the mercy

Jesus shows when looking at the tax collector. It was a look that forgave that man's sins. Jesus, overcoming the resistance of the other disciples, chose him, the sinner and publican, to become one of the Twelve.

Pope Francis — as is known — has always been struck by this look, to the point of drawing his episcopal motto from it in the concise translation that we owe to Bede (672-735). Commenting on the passage of the Gospel, Bede says: "Jesus looked at Matthew with merciful love and chose him — *miserando atque eligendo*" (*Homily* 21).

Among the main passages of the Gospel commented on by the Fathers, the parable of the good Samaritan and Luke's trilogy of mercy (see Lk 10:25-37; 15:1-10; 15:11-24) are particularly significant. In the first, the good Samaritan of humanity is identified with Christ as far back as Origen, and his example must be imitated more with works than with words. It is possible to imitate Christ, the Doctor from Alexandria continues, according to the teaching of Paul: "Be imitators of me, as I am of Christ" (1 Cor 11:1).

For Origen, the Son of God encourages us to perform works of mercy like that performed by the Samaritan. And when he directs his interlocutor to imitate him, he is not speaking to the doctor of law who had questioned him, but to each of us. If people do so, then they will receive eternal life in Jesus Christ (see *Homilies on the Gospel of Luke* 34.3; 34.9). In the parables of the lost sheep, the lost coin, and the forgiving father, God's patient mercy is stressed for that which has been lost — that is, for man the sinner — along with the Father's joy when man is found again and forgiven. Each conversion brings joy among the powers of the heavens (see St. Cyril of Alexandria, *Commentary on Luke. Homily* 106; St. Ambrose, *Exposition on the Gospel of Luke* 7.210). In the parable of the forgiving father the reflection on the mercifulness of the Father reaches its height:

"He, the Father," writes St. Ambrose, "runs to you because he already hears you when you reflect inside yourself, in the secret of your heart.... In coming to you there is prescience, in the embrace his mercy" (*Exposition on the Gospel of Luke* 7.229).

To Peter's question on the number of times to grant forgiveness — up to seven times? — Jesus responded: "I do not say to you seven times, but seventy times seven" (Mt 18:22). The Lord had another view with respect to the proposal made by Peter, because "he is mercy in person" (Chromatius of Aquileia, *Commentary on Matthew*, treatise 59.3). Hilary of Poitiers recalls that Jesus teaches that we must pardon without measure or number, and we must think not of how many times we forgive, but stop becoming angry with those who sin against us, as often as the occasion for anger exists.... Forgiving without measure, indeed, assures being forgiven without measure (*Commentary on Matthew* 18.10).

The text of the dialogue between Jesus and Peter is presented in the parable of the unforgiving servant (see Mt 18:23-26). It tells of how a lord forgave a considerable debt from his servant, while the servant did not do the same with another servant who owed him a small sum, but rather sent him to prison. Jesus speaks to us through the words of the Lord: "Should not you have had mercy on your fellow servant, as I had mercy on you?" (v. 33). And he concludes: "So also my heavenly Father will do to every one of you, if you do not forgive your brother from your heart" (v. 35). The example is as clear as its teaching — St. Chromatius again observes (see *Commentary on Matthew*, treatise 59.3) that we are called on to be merciful, because mercy has been used toward us. And it is not enough to use mercy toward those who please us. The truly merciful person is he who has mercy on his enemy, and does good according to what is written: "Love your enemies, do good to those who hate you" (Lk 6:27). Indeed, God sends his rain not only to those who please him, but also those who displease him, so it is said: "Be merciful, even as your Father is merciful" (Lk 6:36).

An anonymous author, who speaks for many ancient Christians, says: "Such a person is truly blessed, for if in fact he hasn't sinned — which is difficult among men — God's grace helps him along in increasing his sense of justice. So he prays 'Forgive me my debts, just as I too forgive my debtors (Mt 6:12).'" (*Anonymous Commentary on Matthew. Homily* 9, 59)

"Our Father": The Prayer of Mercy

In ancient Christian times, Christian education on mercy found a daily space in the commentary on the request in the Lord's Prayer: "Forgive us our debts" (Mt 6:12, NABRE). The Lord's Prayer (the Our Father) was used in the Latin Christian communities as a synthesis of the catechesis on prayer for those to be baptized through two rites: the delivery of the Lord's Prayer to the person, and the return of that prayer (in Latin, the rites of *traditio/redditio orationis dominicae*). The rite of delivery involved the reading of each request in the prayer with a brief explanation; the rite of return was the recital by memory of the Lord's Prayer by the candidate.

Its principal meaning was to help the new Christian have a permanent conversation with God our Father to ask him to be able to observe the baptismal promises, professed with the Creed. In that context, with the request "forgive us our debts," the catechumen was educated to live by mercy. That prayer expressed the possibility for the new candidate to Christianity to always be able to turn to God in the daily failings of existence, to always be able to start over. For the Fathers of the Church, that education constituted the summary of Jesus' message. What in fact can a human heart hope for, a heart that is born to live eternally with God, if not an immense pity for its always-open wounds, and the mercy of God, who by bandaging them heals them, thus helping it to continue living?

The commentaries on the request in the Lord's Prayer, "Forgive us our debts" (among the best known in the Church are the commentaries of Tertullian, Origen, St. Cyprian, and St. Augustine), were written so that hope would be taken on by each believer and by each person called to the Christian faith. St. Cyprian of Carthage wrote: "How necessary, provident, and beneficial for us to be admonished that we are sinners, who are compelled to plead for our sins, so that, while indulgence is sought from God, the soul is recalled to a consciousness of its guilt! But if we acknowledge our sins, the Lord is faithful and just to forgive us our sins. In his epistle he has combined both, that we should both plead for our sins and that we should obtain indulgence when we plead. Therefore, he said that the Lord was faithful to forgive sins, preserving the faith of his promise, because he who taught us to pray for our debts and our sins promised that mercy and forgiveness would follow."

The catechesis on the Lord's Prayer for persons to be baptized had two principal purposes: to educate new Christians to become aware of the reality of each person, who all need mercy, and of belonging to the Christian community; a Church made up of people that collects them from all areas as they are and educates them to God's mercy for human beings and to mutual mercy, which means the hope of a justified faith in always being able to recover from one's own baptismal failings, of any nature and severity.

St. Augustine encouraged the candidates for baptism in his sermon on the Lord's Prayer: "Listen ... all your sins will be forgiven: that which you received coming into life with original sin, for which together with the children you run to the Savior's grace; and whatever evil you have done in life, with words, deeds, and thoughts. All will be forgiven" (*Sermon* 56, 9.13).

In the life of the Christian, the consciousness of evil, of possible failure, that everyone carries inside, translates into relationships of mercy and mutual help in freeing ourselves from the evil that we encounter daily, thus not lingering more than necessary in judging, which creates negative relationships with our fellow human beings. Mercy leads us to meet on the human level that unites us. People with mercy no longer act under the forces of evil (judging, hating, killing), but looking at themselves and discovering that they are sinners, they pray together, "Forgive us our debts."

This invocation of the Lord's Prayer was taught to the catechumen so that he would pray daily with the faith that human beings can always turn to God, because he, mercy, is on the side of those who fall, reviving them from generation to generation. In the prison of the human heart, devoid of light, God's compassionate, merciful, paternal gaze always descends to illuminate the heart with his light; he does not place people in front of their sins, but by forgiving them introduces the warmth of the embrace of his light.

Therefore, Christians were educated to the daily possibility of being forgiven, of receiving a gesture of mercy, necessary for human beings, as bread is for life, and water for thirst. Without that possibility the very generosity of God would be senseless, because as Tertullian explained, human beings would find themselves in the condition of an ox destined to be killed. He writes: "Having considered God's generosity, we pray next for his indulgence. For, of what benefit is food if, in reality, we are bent on it like a bull on his victim? Our Lord knew that he alone was without sin. Therefore, he taught us to say in prayer: 'Forgive us our debts.'"

Mercy in the Liturgy

The prayers of the liturgy, throughout the liturgical year

and in the sacraments, transmit the Lord's immense mercy, both as a memory of the Savior's gestures of salvation and as a sacrament and example of daily Christian life. Indeed, the liturgy, by including the entire life of Jesus Christ from birth to ascension, winds from generation to generation as a sacrament, just as St. Leo the Great said: "The sacrament of today's holiday belongs to the time of every believer" (*Sermon* 38, 1). Therefore, the liturgical year is indicated by Pope Leo the Great as from Christmas to Pentecost, as the vehicle for communicating salvation to the believers, or the "never-ceasing calls of God's mercy." In a sermon to the people he explained: "On all days and seasons, indeed, dearly beloved, some marks of the Divine goodness are set, and no part of the year is destitute of sacred mysteries, in order that, so long as proofs of our salvation meet us on all sides, we may the more eagerly accept the never-ceasing calls of God's mercy" (*Sermon* 49, 1).

St. Cyril of Jerusalem explained in his catechetical lectures: "We did not really die, we were not really buried, we were not really crucified and raised again; but our imitation was in a figure, and our salvation in reality. Christ was actually crucified, and actually buried, and truly rose again; and all these things he has freely bestowed upon us, that we, sharing his sufferings by imitation, might gain salvation in reality" (*Mystagogical Cathechesis*, 2, 4-6).

The texts of the liturgy express the revelation of Jesus, preserved for us by John the Evangelist: "For God so loved the world that he … sent the Son into the world, not to condemn the world, but that the world might be saved through him" (Jn 3:16-17). For example, the Triduum liturgy of Holy Week transmits the mercy of the Savior in a particularly concentrated way, allowing us to participate in his passion. Regarding baptism, St. Cyril of Jerusalem explains: "We know that baptism, as it purges our sins, and ministers to us the gift of the Holy Spirit, so also it is the counterpart of the sufferings of Christ. For this cause Paul just now cried aloud and said: 'Do you not know that all of us who have been baptized into Christ Jesus were baptized into his death? We were buried therefore with him by baptism into death.' (Rom 6:3-4a)" (*Mystagogical Catechesis* 2.6).

And we come to the Easter Triduum. On *Holy Thursday*, the person who presides over the holy assembly washes, dries, and kisses the feet of the penitent as the sign of reconciliation given back by God and by the community of faith to he who has fallen into some serious failure of Christian faith. In early Christianity, after a period of penitence, on Holy Thursday those repentant were readmitted into the community, and with all of the others they again participated in the Eucharist. It was necessary to reconcile those who had fallen into sin: those who had repudiated or broken the faith professed in baptism, through schism or heresy; or had committed a murder (in the patristic times this also included the crime of abortion and in some areas also that of having killed someone in military service); or had broken the bond of marriage. We know that these sins were subject to public penitence because the lists have been preserved.

The gesture of washing the feet touched the repentant deeply, in a manifest request of mercy from the community of faith, as every participant in the divine liturgy was called on to have mercy on his brother or sister in faith who had violated their baptismal promises. For everyone, the figure of the president of the liturgical assembly stood out as the figure of humble Jesus who bends over me — the repentant — washes me, dries me, puts his hand on my head as a sign of welcoming me, takes me by the hand, raises me up, embraces me, kisses me. The gesture of the forgiving father in the Gospel is repeated. It is as if man said to God, "Why do you love me?" And God, embracing us, responds, "You have returned, my child," and he dries his tears trying to hide them. "I am *mercy*."

The Milanese liturgy was so taken by the gesture of the washing of the feet that it raised it to the level of a sacrament, meaning a gesture of salvation left to the Christian community by the Savior himself. Holy Thursday also recalls the gesture of the gift of Jesus resurrected in the Eucharist, becoming our holy bread that nourishes us and becomes our spiritual offering, because it is the bread of the mercy of the heart of Christ. The repentant sat at everyone's table, the table of the Eucharist.

On *Good Friday*, the community of believers recalls the supreme gesture of Jesus giving his life to the point of dying for us on the cross. The cross, in fact, is the place of life where the Father has mercy for poor humanity, through the Son. Jesus said, "Father, forgive them; for they know not what they do" (Lk 23:34), while he was wounded by the very hand of those he loved. Every loving relationship leaves a door open to vulnerability, to the possibility of being hurt. Remembering this, not fleeing from this vulnerability, already means preparing for the moment of mercy, because we are made for life, even if at times we seek death. All of this entails knowing how to yield to the tenderness of Christ, who, covered in blood, comes to us in his mercy to embraceuse.

Holy Saturday recalls the descent of Jesus to the underworld, when the Savior brought his mercy to our fathers, taking Adam and Eve by the hand to pull them and all of the others up to life, as depicted in the Church of the Holy Savior in Chora (in present-day Istanbul). On *Easter Sunday*, his mercy spreads over all of humanity, as expressed in the monogram of the *Phos Zoe* cross, symbolizing light and life.

CHAPTER II

St. Augustine:
Preacher of Mercy

St. Augustine felt personally touched by the mercy of God, sensing that God had followed him even when he wandered far from him. After converting to Christianity at the age of approximately thirty-three, St. Augustine wrote *Confessions*, the biography of his conversion, as a song of thanks to God's mercy that had been close to him even when he had strayed from the religion of his mother, Monica. For that reason, we could give *Confessions* the subtitle of "Mercy." In a sermon to the people, St. Augustine confessed that upon leaving the nest before he could fly, he was gathered by divine mercy to be returned to the nest. He wrote with great emotion: "I sought [in the Holy Scriptures] with pride what only humility could allow me to find. How much more blessed are you now, with what confidence and safety do you learn, you who are still young ones in the nest of faith, and receive the spiritual food! Whereas I, wretch that I was, as thinking myself fit to fly, left the nest, and fell down before I flew. But the Lord of mercy raised me up, that I might not be trodden down to death by passers by, and put me in the nest again" (*Sermon* 51, 5-6).

He sensed that God makes himself known precisely through mercy, and he wrote: "He extends his mercy to them that know him, and his righteousness to the upright in heart. He does not extend his mercy to them because they know him, but that they may know him; nor because they are upright in heart, but that they may become so" (*On the Spirit and the Letter*, 7.11).

The bishop of Hippo, realizing that mercy belongs to each person both as a need and as an inalienable capacity, spoke of it in all of his writings, always and whenever he had the opportunity, particularly in his commentary on the 150 Psalms, where it appears continuously. He speaks of the mercy of God and the mercy of man, never satisfied with receiving pity. As bishop, he explained to the faithful the mercy that forgives and the mercy that meets the needs of the poor, and as the intellectual he was he dedicated particular attention to mercy for the labors of those who seek glimmers of truth in order to continue to live, "forced," as St. Augustine said of himself, "to pick my way through intricate and obscure paths" (*On the Holy Trinity*, I, 3.6). The intellectual human being, due to the "webs of reason," as he calls the reasoning from which he is unable to emerge, often lives in the shadow of error, always awaiting that ray of light that, for him, is mercy.

St. Augustine was an intellectual, and as such he experienced the falsity that reason loves to construct and the difficulty of extricating himself from the deceptions of pseudo-arguments. "For how much better," he wrote in *Confessions*, "are the fables of poets and grammarians than these traps! ... by what steps was I brought down to the depths of hell! Toiling and turmoiling through want of Truth, since I sought after you, my God (to you I confess it, who had mercy on me, not as yet confessing), sought after you.... You were more inside me than my most inner part; and higher than my highest" (*Confessions*, 3, 6,11).

Speaking of the mercy to have toward intellectuals, who unfortunately fall into the deception of reason, he wrote regarding a request for condemnation of Manichean intellectuals sent to him: "Be they harsh with you [here he addresses the Manicheans, the misguided Christian intellectuals of that time] those who know not the labors of finding the truth, and how difficult it is to avoid errors ... how many cries are necessary to reach understanding, even in the least part ... be they harsh with you, those who have never been deceived by error.... I, for my part, cannot be so" (*Against the Letter the Foundation*, 2-3).

In studying St. Augustine, who was literally overwhelmed by the experience of God's mercy, which he then transmitted to his contemporaries, we can better comprehend the richness of the word mercy itself. The bishop of Hippo sees mercy as encompassing all of Christianity, of Jesus and the Christians. With the word "heart" he indicates man himself, man in his concrete existence, more or less oriented toward the completion of his being. For St. Augustine, human beings identify with their heart, "their love," as he specifies in the *City of God*. It is not the human being of the conceptual abstractions of the philosophers, but human beings as living historical existence, children of the heritage of Adam and the grace of Christ. For him, posing the problem of the human heart is posing the problem of man himself. Investigating the human heart is equivalent to casting a glance on the depths of his mystery that can be reached only by mercy. In his sermons to the people, as in his writings, St. Augustine is literally entranced by the expressions of Scripture that indicate man as a depth whose heart is an abyss. For that reason, many scholars of Augustinian thought see the word "heart" as the key term of his entire philosophy and theology.

The heart, according to the saintly bishop, is man in his deepest intimacy; it is like man's home, the secret room where he loves to live, to rest, to linger. It is that corner where man loves to converse with man, in the perpetual attempt to grasp the word of himself: who he is, where he comes from, where he is going, where he can meet his God. But descending into the heart, into that secret corner of oneself, means wanting to descend into a deep abyss where no one has ever gone, nor can anyone fully arrive. The heart remains impenetrable to man himself.

Yet St. Augustine, despite stopping before the human heart as if before a shrine, recognizes that man wants to look inside and searches for the path to get there, the light to penetrate that darkness. That light comes to him from the faith that God penetrates the abyss of the human heart. To him everything is visible, every depth reveals its most remote parts. Man then senses that, in order to glance into his own depths, he must look inside with the light of God, with his mercy. He discovers that God carries within him the secret of the mystery of the human heart and has made his dwelling in that heart. With his presence, God heals the penitent heart, accepts the offer of the humble heart, and man hears that voice that God listens to, that pureness of heart where God is seen, and "to find that God from whom to turn away is to fall, to whom to turn back is to rise again, in whom to dwell is to live" (*Soliloquies*, I, 1.3).

Mercy is thus innate in man from his birth, carrying with it the rebellion of the ancestors of humanity against God, that places man in a continuous condition of misery in his days, always exposed to the danger of deceiving himself and dying, because he is pregnant with abysmal indigence that causes in him a permanent state of beggary. He only hopes that some heart recognizes it and does not let him die. His heart's thirst is therefore the mercy for his congenital weakness never fully known, that mysterious weakness that envelops with unconscious fear the beating of the human heart. When mercy invades the heart, man senses that at that moment God is present for him, and he goes outside himself: he approaches God, others, and his own mystery. Thus mercy, together with the truth and grace of Christ, becomes one of the paths by which God approaches the most profound roots of the human world. In Christ the three paths meet, and for man approached by Christ, those paths of God can become paths of man.

In his comments on the Psalms, St. Augustine gives the broadest, most attractive and fascinating synthesis of the experience of mercy. It manifests itself in the consolation that it brings to the human heart: you feel rescued, you feel saved, it fills you with an inner tenderness that moves you to tears. It is a mercy that God never succeeds in holding back, because it is spread like a fertilizing rain, among all peoples and every age of man. Rather, the season of human life is actually the season of God's mercy for the same. Thanks to that mercy there is a bridge between God and human beings, which can never fully be broken over time. God, in fact, has mercy for the just as for the sinner, he is always close to the contrite heart, and never abandons human frailty that risks disintegration.

For that reason, the specific subject of the Church's preaching is divine mercy. Man is led to request mercy of God, rather than to demand it. And God in mercy becomes man's debtor; man becomes the debt collector of his mercy. In the Christian conscience, man's mercy toward his fellow human beings is born from the experience of the gift of mercy received from God. By that mercy man ties himself to every human being, never excluding anyone, without debating the time and appropriateness of the assistance. With mercy man learns to feel united with other human beings, not due to bonds of birth and blood, but based on mercy. St. Ambrose,

St. Augustine's teacher, wrote, "What makes us brethren is not family relations, but mercy" (*Exposition on the Gospel of Luke* 7.84). The tie of mercy, which joins people in new bonds, produces works of mercy, those works that produce justice. When a person rich in mercy has nothing to give someone poor, he gives him his love; his heart thus becomes a relative of he who lives in misery. In that experience, man encounters the best part of his fellow human beings, that humanity not disfigured by evil, and in his fellow humans he recognizes and recovers his own humanity.

In conclusion, for St. Augustine misery is one of the great mediations that allows man to know himself, the mystery of his humanity that links him to his fellow human beings and renews his ties to God. Compassion thus also acquires an anthropological value. It provides an indication to understand who human beings are. Placed next to truth and freedom, for St. Augustine mercy represents the axis of Christian comprehension of man. He experienced mercy as a common good, belonging to all, as a good belonging to man, which when lacking deprives man of his own good that is the relationship with God and his brethren. Thus, to those who asked him what he desired, St. Augustine responded that his hope was to praise the infinite mercy of God, eternally and with everyone, in particular with those whose existence he shared. The prayer, which closes his work *On Two Souls, Against the Manicheans*, wonderfully summarizes his thinking, his anthropological proposal on mercy: "Great God, God omnipotent, God of supreme goodness, I supplicate you, hear my prayer. Now that I have felt your mercy, do not allow those with whom I have lived from boyhood, as if we had only one heart, to dissent from me in your worship" (I, 15.24).

Selected Passages from St. Augustine

On the Meaning of the Word Mercy

I very much wish to address your Holinesses on the subject of being merciful or kindhearted, and its real value. Although I have often experienced how forward you are in every kind of good work, still it is necessary that we should have a word or two on the subject, carefully condensed in summary form. We are to discuss then what being merciful or kindhearted essentially is. It is nothing other than feeling a soreness of heart caught from others. It gets its Latin name, *misericordia*, from the sorrow of someone who is miserable; it is made up of two words, *miser*, miserable, and *cor*, heart. It means being heart sore. So when someone else's misery or sorrow touches and pierces your heart, it's called *misericordia*, or soreness of heart.

And so observe, my brothers and sisters, how all the good works which we perform in our lives are really an expression of being merciful or heart sore. For example, you offer some bread to a hungry man, offer sympathetic kindness from the heart; don't do it contemptuously, or you'll be treating a fellow human being like a dog. So when you perform a work of mercy, if you're offering bread, feel sorry for the hungry; if you're offering drink, feel sorry for the thirsty; if you're handing out clothes, feel sorry for the naked; if you're offering hospitality, feel sorry for the stranger and traveler; if you're visiting the sick, feel sorry for the people who are ill; if you're burying the dead, feel sorry for the deceased; if you're patching up a quarrel, feel sorry for the quarrelers.

We do none of these things, if we love God and our neighbor, without some sorrow of heart. (*Sermon* 358A)

Mercy in Words

With our tongue we pray to God, we ingratiate him, we praise him, harmonized together we sing to God; with our tongue every day either we use mercy in speaking with others or we give advice.... Take note: "I held my tongue, as long as the ungodly was in front of me." In front of you is an impudent person, he insults you, says things from another world. Hold your tongue. "I said: I will watch over my ways to not sin with my tongue." Let him speak. You listen and be quiet. One of the two: either he says the truth or he says what is false. If he says the truth, you are the reason. And perhaps this is mercy, because, while you do not want to hear what you did, God, who cares for you, through another tells you what you did, so that, at least confused due to shame, you finally go to seek the medicine. So do not return evil for evil. Because you know not who and what speaks to you through that person. Therefore if he reproaches you for something you have done, acknowledge that you have found mercy, or thinking that you had forgotten or concluding that you are told so that you have shame.... Do not believe that you can appear to be a saint if no one tries you. You are saintly when you are not upset with insults, when you feel sorrow for he who speaks them, when you worry not for your suffering but are pained for him who makes you suffer. All of this is mercy. You feel sorrow because he also is your brother, because he is a member of you. He lashes out against you, he struggles, he becomes sick ... be saddened, do not rejoice. Rejoice only for the tranquility of your conscience. For the rest, be sad. Because you too are a human being. This is the mercy of God. Thus the Lord, with his usual mercy, will allow us, through your prayers, to go deeper (how to speak, how to react), because it is fairly difficult. Now God the Father speaks to you: "I tell you, O soul that I made, O man that I created, I tell you: you were done. What does this mean: you were done? You had perished. But I sent you one who searched for you, I sent you one who walked with you, I sent you one who forgave you. He walked with the feet and pardoned with the hands. Thus when he rose after the resurrection, he showed his hands, his side and his feet: the hands, with which he gave the forgiveness of sins, the feet, with which he announced peace to the outcasts, the side, from which gushed the price of the redeemed." Here then … the "end of the law is Christ for the justification of whoever believes. Let me know my end, Lord." Here then, now you know your end.

And how was it made known to you? Your end was poor, your end was humble, your end was slapped, your end was soiled with spit, false witness was given against your end. And "I held my tongue, as long as the ungodly was in front of me." For you he became the way. "He who says he lives in Christ must act as he acted." He is the way. Now we walk; we are not afraid; we do not lose ourselves. We do not walk outside of the path. Because it is said: "Around the road they placed obstacles, around the road they laid traps." And here is mercy: so that you fall not into the traps, you have mercy itself as the path. (*Sermon* 16A)

The Sweetness of Mercy

"Lord, hear my prayer, because your mercy is sweet." Explain the reason he should be satisfied: because sweet is the mercy of God. But would it not have been more logical to say, Lord, hear my prayer, so that your mercy is sweet for me? For what reason does he say, "Lord, hear my prayer, because your mercy is sweet?" He already stressed with other words the sweetness of the Lord's mercy when, in the middle of the tribulation, he said, "Lord, hear my prayer, because I suffer." And truly, saying, "Lord, hear my prayer, because I suffer," he explains the reason for which he implores to be satisfied. But for the man in the middle of tribulation God's mercy cannot appear to be sweet. Of this sweetness of God's mercy note what Scripture says elsewhere: "Like the rain in the drought, so magnificent is the mercy of God in tribulation." There it said "magnificent"; here it says "sweet." The same bread would not be sweet if it were not preceded by hunger. Thus when the Lord allows or makes it so that we find ourselves in tribulation, also then he is merciful. He does not deny us nourishment, but lights our desire. Why then does he say, "Lord, hear my prayer, because your mercy is sweet?" Hear my prayer without delaying longer: I find myself in a tribulation so great that for me your mercy is sweet. This is why you delayed your help: so that it would be sweet for me. Well, now delay no more: my tribulation has reached the limit; the measure of suffering is full. Thus come your mercy to benefit me. "Lord, hear my prayer, because your mercy is sweet. Look towards me based on the multitude of your mercies, not the multitude of my sins." (*Sermon* 2.1)

Mercy as an Act of Love

The man that has two children is God who has two peoples: the older child is the people of the Jews, the younger is the people of the pagans. The substances received from the Father are the soul, intelligence, memory, ingenuity, and all of the faculties that God gave us to know him and adore him. Having received this heritage, the younger son "went to a far land" — that is, he came to forget his Creator.... He ultimately realized the situation he had fallen into, what he had lost, whom he had offended, and to whose power he had cast himself, "and he came to himself"; first he came to himself and then he returned to the father. Perhaps he said: "My heart has abandoned me"; for this reason it was necessary for him first to come to himself and thus to recognize that he was far away from the father.... He arose, and he returned; in fact, he had stopped where he lay after his fall.

The father sees him at a distance and runs to him.... "And you forgave the impiety of my heart." How close is God's pardon to those who confess their sins! God is, in fact, close to those who have a contrite heart.... While the son was still preparing to tell the father what he repeated to himself: "I will arise, and go to my father, and I will say to him," since the father saw his son's resolve at a distance, he ran to him. What does "run to" mean if not to grant forgiveness in advance? "Yet at a distance," the Gospel says, "the father ran to him, and had compassion."

Why was he moved by compassion? Because the son was exhausted by misery. "He ran to him and embraced him," meaning he threw his arms around his neck. The Father's arm is the Son; he gave him the possibility to bear Christ: this weight does not oppress, it uplifts. "My yoke," says Christ, "is easy and my burden light." The father was bent over the son, not allowing him to fall again.... Thus by embracing the son, the father raised him up, he did not oppress him; he honored him. Yet how is man able to bear God, if not because it is God who bears while he is borne?

The father then orders the best robe to be brought, that Adam had lost sinning. After having welcomed the son with forgiveness and having kissed him, he orders the robe to be brought — that is, the hope of immortality through baptism. And he orders that a ring — the token of the Holy Spirit — be put on his hand, and shoes on his feet, for the readiness to announce the evangelical message of peace, so that the feet of he who brings the good news would be fair. God does that through his servants, through the ministers of the Church. Do they perchance give their own robe, ring, and shoes? They must only provide a service, perform a duty; those goods are given by Him from whose mysterious bosom and treasure they are brought out.... "All that is mine," says the Father to his elder son, "is yours." If you are a promoter of peace, if you reconcile, if you rejoice in the return of your brother, if our banquet does not make you sad, you will not remain outside of the house even though you have already returned from the fields, "all that is mine is yours. We must make merry and be glad," because

"Christ died for the ungodly" and rose up. This is what that statement means: "Your brother was dead, and is alive; he was lost, and is found." (*Sermon* 112)

——

Return to yourself: and, once you are in yourself, look up again, do not remain in yourself. First return to yourself from the outside world, and then give yourself to he who created you, and sought you, lost; he found you, fugitive; he converted you, who had turned your back to him. Thus return to yourself, and move towards he who created you. Imitate that younger son, because maybe it is you.... "He came to himself and said: I will arise." Thus he had fallen. "I will arise," he said, "and go to my father." He who has found himself already renounces himself. How does he renounce? Listen: "And I will say to him: I have sinned against heaven and before you." He renounces himself. "I am no longer worthy to be called your son...."

Listen also to the apostle Paul who denies himself: "But far be it from me to glory except in the cross of our Lord Jesus Christ, by which the world has been crucified to me, and I to the world." Listen to him insist on denying himself. He says, "It is no longer I who live." It is clear he renounces his self; but here follows a triumphant testimony of Christ: "But Christ lives in me." So what does "renounce yourself" mean? To not be your own life. And what does this mean, "to not be your own life"? To do not your will, but the will of he who lives in you. (*Sermon* 330)

Christ is Mercy

So let us sing, brothers and sisters, let us sing: "I will bless the Lord who gave me the gift of intellect." He made a gift of nature, he made a gift of intellect; he restored nature, he restored intellect. The charitable Samaritan who came to our aid used both nature and intellect: he wrapped our wounds, he washed them with wine — and we know what wine — he cared for the creature, he brought it into the inn to be accommodated by those who lived there. The inn is the Church; the Holy Spirit lives there. He dropped from his torn bag the money with which he paid our host for us, the poor; the host received the money, provided care with his oil, spread his ointment on the wounds of sick nature, and healed it; he lit his oil to illuminate our shadows and brought light to our intellect. If you do not have this faith, there will be no Samaritan for you, and you will die from your wounds, having refused the hand that heals you. (*Sermon* 365)

———

Thus did the Lord to the Jews, when they brought him the adulteress, and they set a trap to test him, but ended up themselves falling into the trap. They said: "This woman has been caught in the act of adultery. Now in the law Moses commanded us to stone such. What do you say about her?" They attempted to capture the Wisdom of God in a double trap: if he had ordered to kill her, he would have lost his fame as gentle; while if he had ordered to free her, they could slander him as a violator of the law.

He therefore responded without saying, kill her; nor saying, free her; but saying, "Let him who is without sin among you be the first to throw a stone at her." The law is just that orders the killing of the adulteress; but this just law must have innocent ministers. You who accuse her, that you bring here, look also at who you are. "But when they heard it, they went away, one by one, beginning with the eldest, and Jesus was left alone with the woman standing before him," she who was wounded, and the doctor remained, "the great misery and the great mercy remained."

Those who had brought her were ashamed, but they did not request forgiveness; she who had been brought showed that she was confused, and was healed. "Jesus said to her, 'Woman, has no one condemned you?' She said, 'No one, Lord.' And Jesus said, 'Neither do I condemn you; go, and do not sin again.'" Did Christ act against his law? Indeed his Father had not given the Law without the Son. If the heaven and the earth and all of the things in them were made through him, how can the Law be written without the Word of God? God does not thus act against his law, since neither the emperor acts against his laws, when he grants indulgences to those who have confessed. Moses is the minister of the law, but Christ is the announcer of the law; Moses stones as judge, Christ shows indulgence as king. God thus had pity for the woman due to his great mercy, as here the psalmist prays, as he asks, as he exclaims and cries; which those who had brought the adulteress to the Lord did not want to do: with the words of the doctor they recognized their wounds, but they did not ask for medicine. So there are many who are not ashamed to sin, but are ashamed to repent. O incredible folly! You are not ashamed of the wound, but you are ashamed of the bandages on the wound? Is it not more rank and putrid when it is naked? Thus trust in the doctor, convert, cry out, "I recognize my iniquity and my sin is always before me."

And they all left. Only he and she remained; the Creator and the creature remained; misery and mercy remained; she remained who was aware of her crime, and he remained who forgave the sin. And it is precisely that which he, bending down, wrote on the ground. When man sins, he is told, "You are dirt." Therefore, in granting forgiveness to the sinner, he was giving it to her by writing on the ground. He gave her forgiveness, but in giving it, turning his face toward her, he said, "No one has condemned you?" And she did not respond: "Why? What did

I do, Lord? Did I do something wrong?" She did not respond so, but said, "No one, Lord."

She accused herself. The others were unable to bring proof, and they ran off. But she confessed; her Lord did not ignore her guilt, but searched for faith and confession. "Has no one condemned you?" And she said, "No one, Lord." No one, to confess your sin, Lord, to await forgiveness. "No one, Lord." I acknowledge both things: I know who you are and who I am. And before you I confess. I have in fact heard, "Celebrate the Lord, because he is good." I acknowledge what I confess; I acknowledge your mercy. She said, "I will watch over my ways to not sin with my tongue." The others, acting with deceit, sinned; she, however, by confessing, found forgiveness. "Has no one condemned you?" And she: "No one." That is all. Once more he wrote. He wrote two times, we heard, two times he wrote: first to give forgiveness, then to renew the laws. Both are in fact done when we receive forgiveness. The emperor signed. But since the formalities continue, it is as if he had renewed the laws. And the laws are those that in the first reading we heard from the apostle who commands us to charity. We heard it in the first reading. On this subject the Lord always says: "You shall love the Lord your God with all your heart, and with all your soul, and with all your strength; and you shall love your neighbor as yourself. On these two commandments depend all the law and the prophets." (*Sermon* 16A)

Christians: Members of the Merciful Body of Christ

When Christ speaks, he speaks sometimes in the Person of the head only; which is the Savior himself, born of the Virgin Mary: sometimes in the person of his body, which is the Holy Church, dispersed through all the world. And we ourselves are in his body, if, that is, our faith be sincere in him; and our hope be certain, and our charity fervent. We are in his body; and members of his; and we find ourselves to be speaking in that passage, according to the apostle's sayings, "For we are members of his body"; and this the apostle says in many passages. For if we were to say that they are not the words of Christ, those words, "My God, my God, why has thou forsaken me?" will also not be the words of Christ. For there too, you have, "My God, my God, why has thou forsaken me? The words of mine offences are far from my health." Just as here you have, "from the fact of my sins," so there also you have, "the words of my offenses." And if Christ is, for all that, without sin, and without offenses, we begin to think those words in the Psalm also not to be his. And it is exceedingly harsh and inconsistent that the Psalm should not relate to Christ, where we have his passion as clearly laid open as if it were being read to us out of the Gospel. For there we have, "They divided his garments among them by casting lots." Why did the Lord himself pronounce in his own person the first verse of the Psalm, and say: "My God, my God, why has thou forsaken me?" What would he convey to us, except that the entire Psalm relates to him, as he pronounced it in his own person? Now when it goes on to say, "The words of mine offenses," it is beyond a doubt that they are the words of Christ. Then, from where come "the sins," but from the body, which is the Church? Because both the head and the body of Christ are speaking. Why do they speak as if one person only? Because "they both," as he has said, "shall be one flesh. This (says the apostle) is a great mystery; but I speak concerning Christ and the Church." Then also when he himself was speaking in the Gospel, in answer to those who had introduced a question concerning the putting away of a wife, he says: "Have you not read that which is written, that from the beginning God made them male and female, and a man shall leave father and mother, and cleave to his wife, and they both shall be one flesh. Wherefore they are no more two, but one flesh." If therefore he himself has said, "They are no more two, but one flesh," what wonder if, as they are but "one flesh," they should have but one tongue, and the same speech, as being but "one flesh," the head and the body? Let us listen to them then as being one person; but yet let us hear the head as the head, and the body as the body. The persons are not separated: but their dignities are distinguished; because the head saves, the body is saved: it belongs to the head to show mercy, to the body to mourn over misery; the office of the head is to cleanse, the duty of the body, to confess sins; yet they have but one speech, in which it is not written when it is the body that speaks, and when the head; but we indeed, while we hear it, distinguish the one from the other; he however speaks as but one. For why should he not say, "My sins," who said, "I was hungry, and you gave me no meat; I was thirsty, and you gave me no drink; I was a stranger, and you took me not in. I was sick and in prison, and you visited me not." Assuredly the Lord was not in prison. Why should he not say this, to whom when it was said, "When did we see you hungry, and thirsty, or in prison; and did not minister unto you?" He replied, that he spoke thus in the person of his body, "As you did it to the least of these my brethren, you did it to me…" Why should he not say, "From the face of my sins," who said to Saul, "Saul, Saul, why do you persecute me," who, however, being in heaven, now suffered from no persecutors? But, just as, in that passage, the head spoke for the body, so here too the head speaks the words of the body, while you hear at the same time the accents of the head itself also. Yet when you hear the voice of the body, do not separate the head from it; nor the body, when you hear the voice of the head, "because they are no more two, but one flesh." (*Exposition on Psalm 38*)

The Works of Mercy

He (God) will be the port where our labors will end: we will see God and we will praise God. Then we will no longer say: arise, work, clothe the servants, clothe yourself, adorn yourself with purple, distribute the food to the servants, be careful that the lamp does not go out, be alert, wake up at night, open your hand to the poor, wind [the thread] from the distaff on the spindle. There will be no more works imposed by necessity where there will be no necessities. There will be no works of mercy because there will be no misery. You will not have to break bread for the poor where no one begs. You will not have to host the pilgrim where everyone lives in their native land. You will not have to visit the sick where everyone is eternally well. You will not have to clothe the naked where everyone is clothed with eternal light. You will not have to bury the dead where everyone will live without end. (*Sermon 37*)

———

They break not bread for the hungry, they clothe not the naked, they take not in the stranger, they visit not the sick, they unite not the contentious, they bury not the dead; for these are works of mercy, and up there, there will be no misery for mercy to be shown to. (*Exposition on Psalm 148*)

———

But the souls that thirst after you, and that appear before you (being by other bounds divided from the society of the sea), you water by a sweet spring, that the earth may bring forth her fruit, and you, Lord God, so commanding, our soul may bud forth works of mercy "according to their kind," loving our neighbor in the relief of his bodily necessities, "having seed in itself according to its likeness," when from feeling of our infirmity we [are] compassionate so as to relieve the needy; helping them, as we would be helped; if we were in like need; not only in things easy, as in herb yielding seed, but also in the protection of our assistance, with our best strength, like the tree yielding fruit. (*Confessions*, 13, 17-21)

———

Next follows, "His seed shall be mighty upon earth." The apostle witnesses that the works of mercy are the seed of the future harvest when he says, "Let us not be weary in well doing, for in due season we shall reap"; and, again, "But this I say, he who sows sparingly, shall reap also sparingly." But what, brethren, is more mighty than that not only Zacchaeus should buy the kingdom of heaven by the half of his goods, but even the widow for two small coins, and that each should possess an equal share there? What is more mighty, than that the same kingdom should be worth treasures to the rich man, and a cup of cold water to the poor?... But there are persons who do these things, while they are seeking earthly possessions, either hoping for a reward from the Lord here, or desiring the praise of men; but, the generation of the right ones shall be blessed; that is, the works of those whose gracious God is the God of Israel, who are right-hearted; now a right heart is not to withstand the Father when he chastens, and to trust him, when he promises; not theirs, whose feet are moved away, whose treadings go astray and slip, as it is sung in another Psalm, while they are grieved at the wicked, seeing the ungodly in such prosperity, and imagine that their works perish, because a perishable reward is not given them. But that man who fears God, and who by the conversion of an upright heart is fitted for a holy temple of God, neither seeks the glory of men, nor lusts for earthly riches. But nevertheless, "Glory and riches shall be in his house." For his house is his heart, where, with the praise of God, he lives in greater riches with the hope of eternal life, than with men flattering, in palaces of marble, with splendidly adorned ceilings, with the fear of everlasting death. "For his righteousness endures for ever": this is his glory, there are his riches. While the other's purple, and fine linen, and grand banquets, even when present, are passing away; and when they have come to an end, the burning tongue shall cry out, longing for a drop of water from the finger's end.

"Merciful, pitying, and just is the Lord God." It delights us that he is "merciful and pitying," but it perhaps terrifies us that the Lord God is "just." Fear not, despair not at all, happy man, who fears the Lord, and has great delight in his commandments; be you sweet, be merciful and lend. For the Lord is just in this manner, that he judges without mercy him who has not shown mercy; but, "Sweet is the man who is merciful and lends": God will not spew him out of his mouth as if he were not sweet. "Forgive," he says, "and you shall be forgiven; give, and it shall be given unto you." When you forgive so that you may be forgiven, you are merciful; when you give so that it may be given unto you, you lend. For though all be called generally mercy where another is assisted in his distress, yet there is a difference where you spend neither money, nor the toil of bodily labor, but by forgiving what each man has sinned against you, you gain free pardon for your own sins also. These two offices of kindness, of forgiving sins, are in the passage of the Gospel: "Forgive, and you shall be forgiven; give, and it shall be given unto you."

He, therefore, who does these things "shall guide his words with discretion." His deeds themselves are the words whereby he shall be defended at the Judgment; which shall not be without mercy unto him, since he has himself shown mercy. "For he shall never be moved": he who, called to the right hand, shall hear these words, "Come, O blessed of my Father, inherit the kingdom prepared for you from the foundation of the world." For no works of theirs, save works of mercy, are there mentioned. He therefore shall hear, "Come, O blessed of my Father." (*Exposition on Psalm* 112)

Mercy and the Judgment of Conscience

These are the words of the apostle: "Attend to your salvation with fear and trepidation." [You could respond]: What do you mean I should attend to this salvation with fear and trepidation, given that I am able to attend to my salvation?... "It is God who works in you," therefore: with fear and trepidation. Because that which the humble obtains, the proud person loses. If it is God who works in you, why was it said, "Attend high to your salvation"? Because God acts in us in a way that we also must act. "Be my help": this means that man must also act, while he asks for help. "But good will," he says, "is mine." I admit it is yours. But even if it is yours, who gave it to you? What inspires it? Do not listen to my words, question the apostle: "It is God in fact," he says, "who works the will in you," who works — I repeat — the will, "and the work, consistent with good will...."

"You who judge the earth...." One judges his peer, a person another person, a mortal another mortal, a sinner another sinner. If we were to place first the Lord's sentence: "Let him who is without sin among you be the first to throw a stone," would there not be an earthquake for whoever judges the earth? Let us reflect on that passage of the Gospel. The Pharisees, in order to test the Lord, brought before him a woman who had been caught in adultery. The penalty for that sin was established by the law, by the law, that is, given through Moses, servant of God. With this tricky and fraudulent dilemma the Pharisees addressed the Lord: if he ordered the accused woman to be stoned, he would go against mercy. If, on the other hand, he ordered what the law prohibited, he would be accused of neglecting the law.... In the case of the adulteress he questioned his questioners, and thus he judged his judges. "I do not prohibit," he said, "the stoning of the woman the law orders be stoned, but I ask who is to stone her. I do not oppose the law, but I seek an enforcer of the law." To conclude, listen: "You want to stone her in accordance with the law? Let him who is without sin be the first to throw a stone."

While he was listening to those words, "he wrote with his finger on the ground" to teach the ground. In speaking those things to the Pharisees, he raised his eyes, he looked at the ground and made it tremble. Then, after having spoken, he again wrote on the ground. But they, confused and trembling, went away one by one. O earthquake, where the ground has moved so much as to even change place!

When they had left, the sinner remained with the Savior. The sick person and the doctor remained. Misery remained with mercy. And looking at the woman, he said, "Has no one condemned you?" She said, "No one, Lord." But she was still distraught. The sinners dared not condemn her; they dared not stone the sinner, because upon examining themselves, they found that they were similar to her. But the woman was still in grave danger, because before her remained the judge without sin.

"Has no one," he said, "condemned you?" She said, "No one, Lord": If you also do not condemn me, I am saved. The Lord spoke strongly to this silent anguish: "Neither do I condemn you." Neither do I, although without sin, neither do I condemn you. Conscience had dissuaded the others from revenge, mercy led me to come to your aid....

Perhaps you wish to be useful to others in various human situations.... To serve justice, do not spare money. First be the judge inside yourself and for yourself. First judge yourself, so that, quietly in the secret of your conscience, you can deal with others. Return to yourself, take care of yourself, examine and listen to yourself. There I want to see you a just judge, where you seek not witnesses. You want to proceed with authority so that one tells you of another what you do not know. First judge inside yourself. Did your conscience tell you nothing of yourself? If you do not wish to deny it, yes, it told you something. I do not want to know what it said; you judge, you who listened.

It told you what you have done, what you have received, in what you have sinned. I would like to know what judgment it issued. If you listened well, if you listened righteously, if in listening to yourself you were just, if you climbed up to the court of your conscience, if you suspended yourself on the balance of the heart, if you made use of the severe executioners of fear: you listened well if you listened so, and without doubt you have punished sin, repenting. Now, you discussed the case, you listened, you judged. And yet you saved yourself. In the same way listen to your neighbor, if you learn as the Psalm recommends: "Be wise, you who judge the earth...."

If you listen to your neighbor as you listen to yourself, you will prosecute the sins, saving the sinner. And if someone, disregarding the fear of God, were insensitive in correcting himself from sins, you will prosecute this [attitude], you will attempt to correct it, you will attempt to destroy and eliminate it with every effort so that, the sin condemned, the person will be saved. There are two names: person and sinner. God made people; people made themselves sinners. What people have done [shall] be destroyed, what God has done shall be freed ... with the disposition of one who loves, with the disposition of one who corrects. (*Sermon* 13, 3-5.7.8)

The Lord Gives Himself to Man in Mercy

The Lord rose to heaven revealing himself in the presence of his disciples. This we know, this we believe, this we declare. "He made a gift to human beings." What gifts? The Holy Spirit. Who gives such a gift, what type of person is he? Great indeed is God's mercy; he gives a gift equal to himself, because the gift is the Holy Spirit, and the entire Trinity, the Father and the Son and the Holy Spirit are a single God. Who gives us the Holy Spirit? Listen to the apostle: "The love of God," he says, "was poured into our hearts." How, O beggar, do you know that the love of God was poured into man's heart? "We have such a treasure in earthen vessels," he says. Why in "earthen vessels"? "To show that the transcendent power comes from God." Last, after having said, "The love of God was poured into our hearts," so that everyone would not believe he has by himself the means with which to love God, he immediately added, "it was given to us through the Holy Spirit." Therefore, so that you may love God, so that God may dwell in you, and love what is yours; that he may give you impulse, set you on fire, raise you to his love. (*Sermon* 128)

———

Hear, therefore, these words, and say you with him, "Have pity upon me, O God, after your great mercy." He that implores great mercy confesses great misery. Let them seek a little mercy of you, that have sinned in ignorance: "Have pity," he says, "upon me, after your great mercy." Relieve a deep wound after your great healing. Deep is what I have, but in the Almighty I take refuge. Of my own so deadly wound I should despair, unless I could find so great a physician. "Have pity upon me, O God, after your great mercy: and after the multitude of your pities, blot out my iniquity." What he says, "Blot out my iniquity," is this, "Have pity upon me, O God." And what he says, "After the multitude of your pities," is this, "After your great mercy." Because great is the mercy, many are the mercies; and of your great mercy, many are your pitying. You do consider mockers to amend them, do consider ignorant men to teach them, do consider men confessing to pardon. Did he this in ignorance? A certain man had done some, many evil things he had done; "Mercy," he said, "I obtained, because ignorant I did it in unbelief." This David could not say, "Ignorant I did it." For he was not ignorant of how very evil a thing was the touching of another's wife, and how very evil a thing was the killing of the husband, who knew not of it, and was not even angered. They obtain therefore the mercy of the Lord that have in ignorance done it; and they that have knowing done it, obtain not any mercy it may chance, but "great mercy."

"More and more wash me from my unrighteousness." What is, "More and more wash"? One much stained. More and more wash the sins of one knowing: you that have washed off the sins of one ignorant. Not even thus is it to be despaired of your mercy. "And from my delinquency purge me." According to the manner in which he is physician, offer a recompense. He is God; offer sacrifice. What will you give that you may be purged? For see upon whom you call; upon a just one you call. He hates sins, if he is just; he takes vengeance upon sins, if he is just; you will not be able to take away from the Lord God his justice: plead mercy, but observe the justice: there is mercy to pardon the sinner, there is justice to punish the sin. What then? You ask mercy; shall sin unpunished abide? Let David answer, let those that have fallen answer, answer with David, and say, no, Lord, no sin of mine shall be unpunished; I know the justice of him whose mercy I ask: it shall not be unpunished, but for this reason I will not that you punish me, because I punish my sin: for this reason I beg that you pardon, because I acknowledge....

"And ungodly men shall to you be converted." So full are you of the wealth of mercy, that for those converted to you, not only sinners of any sort, but even the ungodly, there is no cause for despair. "And ungodly men shall to you be converted." Wherefore? That believing on him that justifies an ungodly man, their faith may be counted for righteousness. (*Exposition on Psalm* 51)

The Ministers of the Church are the Ministers of Mercy

To the extent allowed us by the Lord, who has made us the ministers of his word and of his sacrament to serve you in the overabundance of his mercy, we assume the commitment to examine and explain, as will be possible for us, this Psalm which we just sang, as brief for the number of words, as important for the depth of the concepts: we trust in his help, that as he made you attentive, he will make us suitable for this task. Your soul be alive and awaken, turning to God! The fact is that God set the time of his promises and set the time to fulfill what he promised. The time of the promises was that that goes from the prophets to John the Baptist; that, instead, which proceeds forward until the end, is the time for fulfillment of the promises. And faithful is God, who became our debtor, not because he received something from us, but because he promised such great things to us.

He shall drink of the brook in the way, therefore shall he lift up his head. Let us consider him drinking of the brook in the way: first of all, what is the brook? The onward flow of human mortality: for as a brook is gathered together by the rain, overflows, roars, runs, and by running runs down — that is, finishes its course — so is all this course of mortality. Human beings are born, they live, they die, and when some die others are born, and when they die others are born, they succeed, they flock together, they depart and will not remain. What is held fast here? What does not run? What is not on its way to the abyss as if it was gathered together from rain? For as a river suddenly drawn together from rain from the drops of showers runs into the sea, and is seen no more, nor was it seen before it was collected from the rain; so this hidden rain is collected together from hidden sources, and flows on; at death again it travels where it is hidden: this intermediate state sounds and passes away. Of this brook he drinks, he has not disdained to drink of this brook, for to drink of this brook was to him to be born and to die. What this brook has is birth and death; Christ assumed this, he was born, he died. *Therefore he drank from the brook along the way.* (*Exposition on Psalm* 110).

CHAPTER III

Anthology

***St. Ignatius of Antioch**, in the letter addressed to the Christians of Philadelphia and Rome, while he traveled to the capital of the empire to give the supreme testimony of love for Christ, wrote of his own martyrdom as a sign of divine mercy.*

My brothers, in my abounding love for you I am overjoyed to put you on your guard — though it is not I, but Jesus Christ. Being a prisoner for his cause makes me the more fearful that I am still far from being perfect. Yet your prayers to God will make me perfect so that I may gain that fate which I have mercifully been allotted. (*Letter to the Christians of Philadelphia*, 5, 1)

———

I blush to be reckoned among them, for I do not deserve it, being the least of them and an afterthought. Yet by his mercy I shall be something, if, that is, I get to God. (*Letter to the Christians of Rome*, 9, 2)

St. Clement of Rome, writing in the name of the Roman Church, invited the Christians of Corinth to practice charity and achieve unity. In the great prayer placed at the end of his letter, he glorifies the merciful goodness of God.

Let us yield obedience to his excellent and glorious will; and imploring his mercy and loving kindness, while we forsake all fruitless labors, and strife, and envy, which leads to death. (*Letter to the Christians of Corinth*, 9, 1)

———

You, Lord, did create the earth.
You who are faithful throughout all generations,
righteous in your judgments,
marvelous in strength and excellence,
You who are wise in creating
and prudent in establishing that which you have made,
who are good in the things which are seen
and faithful with them who trust on you,
merciful and compassionate,
forgive us our iniquities and our unrighteousness
and our transgressions and shortcomings.
Lay not to our account every sin of your servants and your
    handmaids
… and guide our steps to walk in holiness of heart.
(*Letter to the Christians of Corinth*, 60, 1-2)

St. Polycarp of Smyrna *wrote to the Christians of Philippi urging them to flee from vice and live an upright life in divine mercy and forgiveness; his advice is particularly addressed to the presbyters who lead the Christian community.*

And let the presbyters be compassionate and merciful to all, bringing back those who wander, visiting all the sick, and not neglecting the widow, the orphan, or the poor, but always providing for that which is becoming in the sight of God and man…. If then we entreat the Lord to forgive us, we ought also ourselves to forgive; for we are before the eyes of our Lord and God, and we must all appear at the judgment-seat of Christ, and must every one give an account of himself. (*Letter to the Philippians*, 6, 1.2)

St. Justin, a Palestinian philosopher martyred in Rome, is the author of some of the best-known apologies of the Christian faith during the second century. In his text he stresses that divine mercy spreads over the just and the unjust without distinction, and invites sincere prayer even for one's enemies.

And in addition to all this we pray for you, that Christ may have mercy upon you. For he taught us to pray for our enemies also, saying, "Love your enemies; be kind and merciful, as your heavenly Father is." For we see that the Almighty God is kind and merciful, causing his sun to rise on the unthankful and on the righteous, and sending rain on the holy and on the wicked. (*Dialogue with Trypho*, 96)

St. Hilary of Poitiers *deals with the issue of Christian forgiveness, commenting on the dialogue between Jesus and Peter in the Gospel of Matthew (Chapter 18).*

When Peter asked him whether he should forgive his brother sinning against him up to seven times, the Lord replied, "Not up to seven times but up to seventy times seven times." In every way he teaches us to be like him in humility and goodness. In weakening and breaking the impulses of our rampant passions he strengthens us by the example of his leniency, by granting us in faith pardon of all our sins. For the vices of our nature did not merit pardon. Therefore all pardon comes from him. In fact, he pardons even those sins that remain in one after confession....

By the gift of baptism he grants the grace of salvation to his revilers and persecutors. How much more is it necessary, he shows, that pardon be returned by us without measure or number. And we should not think how many times we forgive, but we should cease to be angry with those who sin against us, as often as the occasion for anger exists. Pardon's frequency shows us that in our case there is never a time for anger, since God pardons us for all sins in their entirety by his gift rather than by our merit. Nor should we be excused from the requirement of giving pardon that number of times, as prescribed by the Law (see Gn 4:24), since through the grace of the Gospel God has granted us pardon without measure. (*Commentary on Matthew* 18)

St. Basil, *bishop of Caesarea in Cappadocia, speaks in his letters of the Father's joy for the repentant sinner, found again like a lost sheep, and like the prodigal son of the parable from the Gospel of Luke. The heavenly Father feels sorrow for everyone who strays from God, as does the father in the parable, and every conversion brings joy to him and to the entire family of God. There is also a gentle reproach for those who, despite being members of this family, but still too hard of heart, judge others believing they are steadfast in their faith in God, unable to rejoice together with the Father of mercy.*

The good shepherd, who left them that had not wandered away, is seeking after you. If you give yourself to him he will not hold back. He, in his love, will not disdain even to carry you on his own shoulders, rejoicing that he has found his sheep which was lost. The Father stands and awaits your return from your wandering. Only come back, and while you are yet far off, he will run and embrace you, and, now that you are cleansed by repentance, will enwrap you in embraces of love.... "For verily I say unto you," says he, "there is joy in heaven before God over one sinner that repents." If any of those who think they are upright find fault because of your quick reception, the good Father will himself make answer for you in the words, "It was proper to make merry and be glad for this my daughter was dead and is alive again, was lost and is found." (*Letter* 46)

St. Gregory Nazianzen, bishop and Doctor of the Church, and also teacher of St. Jerome, describes works of mercy in a well-known sermon that discusses love for the poor.

"Blessed are the merciful," says Scripture, "for they shall obtain mercy" (Mt 5:7) (Mercy is not low on the list of the beatitudes); it says, "Blessed is he who considers the poor and needy" (Ps 41:1); it says, "It is well with the man who deals generously and lends" (Psalm 112:5); it says, "He is ever giving liberally and lending" (Psalm 37:26). Let us appropriate the beatitude; let us earn a name for thoughtfulness; let us become good. Not even night should interrupt your mission of mercy. "Do not say to your neighbor, 'Go, and come again, tomorrow I will give it'" (Prv 3:28).

Do not let anything come between your impulse to do good and its execution: compassion, this alone, cannot be put off. "Share your bread with the hungry, and bring the homeless poor into your house" (Is 58:7), and do so gladly. "He who does acts of mercy," says Scripture, let him do so "with cheerfulness" (Rom 12:8). The good you do has twice the value when done promptly. What is done in bad grace or under duress is both distasteful and repellent.

Doing good is cause for celebration, not complaint. "If you take away the yoke," says Scripture, "the pointing of the finger and speaking wickedness," what will be the result? What a great and wonderful thing! What a magnificent reward for your actions! "Then shall your light break forth like the dawn, / and your healing shall spring up speedily" (Is 58:8). Is there anyone who does not long for light and healing?

If, then, you place any credence in what I say, servants of Christ and brothers and fellow heirs, while we may, let us visit Christ, let us heal Christ, let us feed Christ, let us clothe Christ, let us welcome Christ, let us honor Christ, not with food alone, like some; nor with ointments, like Mary; nor with the tomb alone, like Joseph of Arimathea; nor with obsequies, like Nicodemus, who loved Christ in half measure; and not with gold and frankincense and myrrh as the Magi did before these others. Rather, since the Lord of all will have "mercy, and not sacrifice" (Mt 9:13) and since a kind heart is worth more than myriads of fat sheep, this let us offer to him through the poor who are today downtrodden, so that when we depart this world they may receive us into the eternal habitations in Christ himself, our Lord, to whom be the glory forever. Amen. (*Sermon* 14, 38,40)

St. Chromatius, the bishop of ancient Aquileia, was active in the fourth and fifth centuries. He is the author of a Commentary on the Gospel of Matthew and of numerous homilies, which are a precious testimony of the faith and vitality of the Church that he presided over with doctrine and charity.

The Lord urges us repeatedly, in both the Old Testament and the New Testament, to practice mercy.

But in this text there is the summary of beatitude to justify our faith: there is in overabundance, because the teaching comes to us from the very voice of the Lord: "Blessed be the merciful, because God shall use mercy with them."

The God of mercies says that the merciful are blessed. With this he intends to say that no one can obtain mercy from the Lord if in turn he has not used mercy. Elsewhere it is said, "Be merciful even as the Father that is in heaven is merciful." (*Commentary on Matthew*, 17.6)

———

"If Cain is avenged sevenfold, truly Lamech seventy-sevenfold" (Gn 4:24).

Peter held that, if a brother had offended him, pardoning him seven times was more than enough. It was the same number as the revenge for Cain!

But the Lord thought otherwise; he is mercy in person; he wants the same criteria that he uses to be used among brothers and sisters; he wants peace and harmony to reign among the brothers and sisters at all costs ... and he gives a clear indication of how dear fraternal charity is to his heart.

If in fact the Son of God, due to his divine goodness, has forgiven us all of our sins, has forgiven us all of the crimes we have committed, has forgiven us as a gift of extraordinary mercy; how much more so we should forgive every failing that a brother may have committed against us!

Thus we can say that we have truly imitated the example that the Lord left us. (*Commentary on Matthew*, 59.3)

St. Ambrose, *bishop of Milan, shows us the heavenly Father who in the image of the father from the parable in Luke, runs to meet his repentant son to give him much more than his repentance could ever lead to hope.*

He runs to you, because he already hears you when you reflect inside yourself, in the secret of your heart. Then when you are still far, he sees you and begins to run. He sees into your heart, he hastens so that no one will keep you, and he embraces you.

In coming to you there is prescience, in the embrace his mercy, and I would say almost the strong sensation of fatherly love!

He embraces you to raise those who lay on the ground, and to ensure that he who was oppressed by the weight of sins and bent towards earthly things, again raises his eyes to the heavens, where to search for his creator.

Christ embraces you, because he wants to remove the weight of slavery from your neck, and set a sweet yoke on you. (*Exposition on the Gospel of Luke*, 7.229-230)

St. John Chrysostom, *originally from Antioch and then patriarch of the imperial capital of Constantinople, and one of the great witnesses of the Gospel until he gave his own life, left us lessons in active mercy through his generosity and constant efforts against all types of misery, whether spiritual or material, of his believers.*

Blessed be the merciful, for they shall obtain mercy.

Here he seems to me to speak not only of those who show mercy in giving of money, but those likewise who are merciful in their actions. For the way of showing mercy is manifold, and this commandment is broad.

What then is the reward thereof?

"For they shall obtain mercy," says Jesus.

And it seems indeed to be a sort of equal recompense, but it is a far greater thing than the act of goodness. For whereas they themselves show mercy as human beings, they obtain mercy from the God of all; and it is not the same thing, man's mercy, and God's; but as wide as is the interval between wickedness and goodness, so far is the one of these removed from the other. (*Homilies on the Gospel of Matthew*, 15.6)

***St. Cyril**, the bishop of Alexandria who played a large part in the successful Council of Ephesus in 431, contrary to many theologians who over the centuries gradually marginalized mercy, places it among many other divine properties, after those considered more important that derive from the metaphysical essence of God. He helps us reflect on how the Fathers clearly felt the central role of mercy in divine revelation.*

Closely neighboring, so to speak, upon the virtues which we have just mentioned is compassion, of which he next makes mention. For it is a most excelling thing, and very pleasing to God, and in the highest degree becoming to pious souls. It may suffice for us to imprint on our mind that it is an attribute of divine nature. "For be merciful," he says, "even as your Father is merciful." (*Commentary on Luke, Sermon* 29)

St. Maximus, *called the "Confessor" because he succeeded in proudly defending Christian orthodoxy with his words, his writings, and his life, describes mercy as God's lenience toward sinners.*

The heralds of the truth and ministers of divine grace, who have explained to us from the beginning right down to our own time each in his own day the saving will of God, say that nothing is so dear and loved by him as when men turn to him with true repentance.

Wishing to show that this is by far the most holy thing of all, the divine word of God the Father (the supreme and only revelation of infinite goodness) deigned to dwell with us in the flesh, humbling himself in a way no words can explain. He said, he did, and he suffered those things which were necessary to reconcile us, while we were yet enemies, with God the Father, and to call us back again to the life of blessedness from which we had been alienated.

Not only did he heal our diseases with his miracles, and take away our infirmities by his sufferings, and, though sinless, pay our debt for us by his death like a guilty man.

He freed us from many, terrible sins. It was also his desire that we should aim to become like himself in love of men and in perfect mutual charity, and he taught us this in many ways. He taught it when he proclaimed, "I came not to call the righteous but sinners, to repentance" (Lk 5:32). And again, "Those who are well have no need of a physician, but those who are sick." (Lk 5:31). He also said that he had come to seek and to save the lost sheep; and on another occasion, that he had been sent to the lost sheep of the house of Israel. In the same way, in the parable of the lost coin, he referred in a symbolic way to the fact that he had come to restore in men the royal likeness which had been lost by the evil-smelling filthiness of passions. Likewise, he said: "Just so, I tell you, there is joy in heaven over one sinner who repents" (Lk 15:7). He taught it when he brought relief, with oil, wine, and bandages, to the man who had fallen among thieves and had been stripped of all his clothing and left half-dead from his injuries. Having placed him on his own beast, he entrusted him to the innkeeper; after paying what was needed for his care, he promised that when he came back he would repay whatever more was spent. Christ is humanity's Good Samaritan.

He taught it when he said that the prodigal son's all-loving father took pity on him and, kissing him as he came running back repentant, clothed him once more with the beauty of his glory, and did not reproach him in any way for what he had done. He taught it when he found the sheep which had strayed from the divine flock of a hundred, wandering over hills and mountains. He did not drive it or beat it, but brought it back to the fold. In his mercy, placing it on his shoulders, he restored it, with compassion, unharmed to the rest of the flock.

He taught it when he cried, "Come to me, all who labor and are heavy laden, and I will give you rest" (Mt 11:28), and "Take my yoke upon you" (Mt 11:29). By "yoke," of course, he meant "commandments" or a life lived according to the principles of the Gospel; by "burden" he meant the labor which repentance seems to involve. "For my yoke," he says, "is easy, and my burden is light" (Mt 11:30). Again, teaching divine righteousness and goodness he commanded, "Be holy, be perfect, be merciful as your heavenly Father is merciful" (Lk 6:36), and, "Forgive and you will be forgiven" (Lk 6:37), and, "Whatever you wish that men would do to you, do so to them" (Mt 7:12). (*Letter 11*)

Isaac of Nineveh, also called the "Syrian," originally from the Persian Gulf and then briefly the bishop of Nineveh, is widely venerated throughout the Christian Orient. Starting with him, this anthology opens to an author from the end of the patristic era and to a Nestorian author, outside of Chalcedonian religious unity that after centuries of clashes and tensions still endured within the borders of the Roman Empire, by then reduced in territory and having its capital on the banks of the Bosphorus. This beautiful text recalls that mercy must go beyond justice, and that the merciful man will not be saved from hardships to enter the kingdom of God, as it was for the Son of God and his disciples.

But I say: if the merciful be not even above justice, he is not merciful. This means that he will not only show mercy unto people on his own part, but that he will voluntarily suffer iniquity with delight, so that he does not maintain and postulate full justice in his dealings with his fellow human beings, but is merciful towards them and surpassing justice by mercy, wreathing for himself the crown not of the just under the law, but of the perfect under the new covenant.

To give the poor from one's own possessions, and to cover the naked on seeing them, to love the neighbor as one self, not to do iniquity or falsehood, are things commanded also by the old law. But perfection in behavior, according to the new covenant, commands more.... The Gospel commands not only to suffer gladly iniquitous dealing in possessions and other outward things, but even to give yourself in behalf of your neighbor. (*Mystic Treatise*, 4)

An anonymous commentator on the Gospel of Matthew advises us not to try to outsmart God. A person who prays and says he forgives but does not forgive is lying to himself. He may pray, but he cannot fool or deceive God, and thus he will not receive forgiveness until he himself has forgiven.

With what assurance does that person pray who harbors animosity toward someone who has offended him? Even as he lies when he prays and says, "I forgive," and does not forgive, so too he seeks pardon from God, but he will not be pardoned.

Therefore, if that person who has been offended prays to God without assurance unless he pardons the very person who offended him, how do you think that person prays who not only has been offended by another but himself offends and oppresses others through injustice?

But many people who are unwilling to forgive those who sin against them avoid saying this prayer. They are ill-advised, first, because the one who does not pray as Christ taught is not Christ's disciple; second, because the Father does not graciously hear a prayer that the Son has not recommended.

For the Father knows the words and meaning of his Son, and he does not accept what the human mind has devised but what the wisdom of Christ has expressed.

Therefore you may indeed say a prayer, but you may not outsmart and deceive God. And you will not receive forgiveness unless you yourself have first forgiven. (*Incomplete work on Matthew, Homily* 14)

This **Ancient "Homily on Holy Saturday"** *is offered to us in the office of readings for Holy Saturday, the day that the Church is silent, still contemplating the death of Jesus and awaiting his resurrection.*

What is happening? Today there is a great silence over the earth, a great silence, and stillness, a great silence because the King sleeps; the earth was in terror and was still, because God slept in the flesh and raised up those who were sleeping from the ages. God has died in the flesh, and the underworld has trembled.

Truly he goes to seek out our first parent like a lost sheep; he wishes to visit those who sit in darkness and in the shadow of death. He goes to free the prisoner Adam and his fellow-prisoner Eve from their pains, he who is God, and Adam's son.

The Lord goes in to them holding his victorious weapon, his cross. When Adam, the first created man, sees him, he strikes his breast in terror and calls out to all, "My Lord be with you all." And Christ in reply says to Adam, "And with your spirit." And grasping his hand he raises him up, saying, "Awake, O sleeper, and arise from the dead, and Christ shall give you light.

"I am your God, who for your sake became your son, who for you and your descendants now speak and command with authority those in prison: Come forth, and those in darkness: Have light, and those who sleep: Rise.

"I command you: Awake, sleeper, I have not made you to be held a prisoner in the underworld. Arise from the dead; I am the life of the dead. Arise, O man, work of my hands, arise, you who were fashioned in my image. Rise, let us go hence; for you in me and I in you, together we are one undivided person.

"For you, I your God became your son; for you, I the Master took on your form; that of slave; for you, I who am above the heavens came on earth and under the earth; for you, man, I became as a man without help, free among the dead; for you, who left a garden, I was handed over to Jews from a garden and crucified in a garden.

"Look at the spittle on my face, which I received because of you, in order to restore you to that first divine inbreathing at creation. See the blows on my cheeks, which I accepted in order to refashion your distorted form to my own image."